...K DIY

AN ETHAN WARES SKATEBOARD SERIES
BOOK 5

MARK MAPSTONE

1
DITCH SPOT

Ethan's burnt orange T-shirt matched the biscuit tanned skin of Simon, the Marketing Director, who wanted him to skate down a slope. Simon was from London, and celebrated his new job at N27 with a status update. He was a doer, who meant business, but he also ate Haribo in his Vauxhall Insignia during lunch. Simon jogged up the hill as if what he had to say was important.

'Okay, guys.' He also liked to clap which he learnt on team-building camp. 'Let's just run through this again. All I need you to do is roll down the hill, arms wide…' He'd planned everything out during a long pub-lunch with an iPad and a pencil balanced on his top lip. '… and skate down past us. Got it?' Thumbs went up like they were spring loaded.

Local grommets had gathered at the bottom of the flyover and were restless whilst waiting for some action. Who could blame them? They'd seen nothing but dumb stuff all afternoon.

The filming was for a series of promotional segments between programmes, except Simon had a funny idea of what skateboarding looked like. Ethan would have been fine filming those segments solo, but for some reason, a second skateboarder was needed and the first available freelancer was Elliott Sommers. And the last person on earth he wanted to be working with was Ethan.

'This is what you do all day?' Elliott hissed.

'Sometimes,' Ethan sighed.

'And there's me thinking you had a sweet job. I couldn't have been more wrong. I'm only here for the money, so don't go thinking we're friends again.'

A siren from a fire appliance slid through the air a mile down the hill. The truck popped out between trees and blinked its blue lights, racing to free a cow from a ditch or rescue a cat from a tree. This morning's breaking news story announced a theft from a chemical distribution centre. Details were still being discovered, but the media behaved as if it was the crime of the century.

Simon noticed Ethan's elbow pads were on the floor.

'They're not needed. We're professionals.'

'You're also role models on national TV.' Simon handed them back and took up his position beside the cameraman again. Ethan put the pads back on as the muppet wasn't worth the battle.

Elliott was still complaining.

'We both agreed to do this,' Ethan said to him. 'So, let's just get it done, then we can get back to some proper skating.'

'*I'll* be proper skating,' Elliott scoffed. '*This* is *your* world, not mine.' That tone was supposed to hurt, but the comment just hung in the air between them, all stained and stinking of Elliott's intensions.

'You can't keep blaming me for a company which would have gone bust anyway.'

'You don't know that,' Elliott said. 'It's so ironic that the biggest loser on the team ended up with the cushy job.'

Simon waved his sheet of paper at the bottom of the slope, and they set off again. He mirrored their entire routine out of frame like a primary school teacher guiding a nativity play. He held his arms wide, faked a wobble, and tried to encourage Ethan to raise his arms, whilst they skidded on their tails, flashed teeth at each other, high-fived, and rolled the rest of the way down the hill.

'Great. That was just perfect.' Simon trotted after them. 'But this time, when you look at each other, really put your heart into it. You're doing what you love, yeah?' Simon clapped his happiness out as they walked back up the hill.

'With any luck, they'll edit me out completely,' Elliott said.

They got back into positions and Simon pointed to Ethan's elbows. Those pads had slipped off again.

The next attempt was only marginally better than the previous, but after bombing the hill Ethan kicked out a powerslide and just missed Simon's ankles.

Simon jumped back out of the way, but Ethan was too far down the hill to hear the abuse thrown at him.

A dark grey old Volvo pulled in under the flyover. Elliott's head dropped as he saw who it was, and his usual dumb sneer slid down to his Etnies. The car door jammed and Elliott's dad needed to kick it, then he struggled to get out of the seat like tall men do when they'd bought from a dealership with limited choice of vehicles. Thin, dirty fingers pulled his crumpled shirt straight and swept back his hair. It made no difference to his appearance.

'I just need a couple of minutes,' Elliott shouted.

'What do you want, boy?'

'I've got this business idea which can make a tonne of money. I've got everything here.' Elliott flashed his phone screen up too quick to get a proper look. 'I wanna buy some boards, but I need to borrow some money.'

His dad listened with a look which said *dumb-idea* and hitched his hands on his hips as if he knew where the story was going. 'How much?'

'I'll put it with the hundred and fifty I'll get from this job then pay you back a hundred a month.'

'How much!' His dad took the phone and squinted into the screen. He was humouring. Building up hope, lifting it high with possibilities where it caught the sun and looked pretty. The crash always killed if the fall was high enough. Ethan could see it, but Elliott couldn't or didn't want to.

'I wanna start a skate company. There's no decent shop for miles and the only choice we've got is run by an idiot. With this, I can buy in bulk, and sell to everyone at a profit. Easy money.'

'How much?!'

'Five-hundred.'

'And then we'll be business partners. How much do I get?'

'No. I mean, it'll just be me. A loan.'

'Then forget it. Get a proper job like everyone else does; one that pays real money.'

Elliott fell from six-stories to his death, right

there. His dad stepped over his son's corpse and climbed back into the car complaining about wasting his time. 'This,' he showed the racing section of the paper with biro blue circles marked. 'Lightning Blue, at 100 to 1. Now that's something worth putting five-hundred on.'

Hope stretched and snapped with that familiar sound of a car pulling away. Ethan made a mental note to ask, one day when things were good between them again, if his dad ever smacked him around too.

'Break time over.' Simon clapped his action-hands like he was directing a pantomime. He needed everyone to stay focused, be more skater-y, extreme, and a bit cooler.

'So, um,' Elliott hesitated. 'If any more jobs like this come up…'

'They pop-up occasionally, but I'll put your name forward.'

That ask hurt judging by the silence as they walked back up the hill.

'Are you really starting a company?'

'The industry isn't coming to me, is it?' Then he swore to himself at the shadow of suck his old man left behind. 'He's got the money. Five-hundred isn't a crazy amount.'

Ethan searched for the right thing to say but it must have looked like pity or something because Elliott took it the wrong way.

'I don't need your help,' Elliott said. 'I just need cash.'

Simon wanted them back up the hill to go again, but the grommets were ready to leave.

'I've a better idea,' Ethan shouted.

2

IMBECILES

'There's a spot down here.' A smooth concrete bank under the flyover had a two-foot-high ledge and new tarmac laid on the run-up. 'This is going to look way better than this hill.' He pointed at the line he'd take along the tarmac. 'If I ride straight up this bank, do a trick on the ledge, and roll back down again. You'll get the shot for your edit, it'll look dangerous enough for the average viewer, plus all the skaters will enjoy it. Get a low camera angle, maybe a second camera setup further back, and with the light coming under the bridge, it'll look golden.'

It was a very different approach to what Simon wanted, but he discussed it with the cameraman who noted the change of angles. Their quiet conversation was unnecessary as there was nothing to discuss: they wouldn't be able to argue with

Ethan's years of watching great edits and directing his own filmers to capture the best angles. Besides he wasn't going to let them turn him into an embarrassment.

'Come on.' Ethan clapped at the director to get a move on. 'Let's give it a try whilst the light is good. Otherwise, we'll lose it.'

Taking charge felt good.

'No more than a couple of tries.' Simon was still reluctant, but the cameraman nodded his approval.

'That's all I need.'

Finally, the kids woke up and looked interested enough to stick around. Something decent was about to happen.

'Want me to follow behind you?' Elliott asked.

'Not for this first attempt.' Ethan tightened a loose truck bolt. It was important to show them the line would work. Fewer people meant less chance of screwing up on the first take. They'd love it, and that would be the right time to bring in a second rider and double up the effect.

Elliott hissed like a snake. 'It looks like *the Flare's* ego is back again.'

The cameraman got into position and Simon gave Ethan his cue to go. Ethan sprinted off towards the bank, threw his board down, and gave another couple of hard pushes. His wheels clacked over the small lip at the bottom and the echo cut through the ambient noise of road traffic all around them. The ride up was short and fast, but just before the nose hit it the ledge, he ollied into a frontside nose-pick, grabbed the rail, and heaved the board back in. The downside of the bank kicked up a fresh plume of dust which carried with him onto the tarmac. The kids had been told to stay quiet whilst the camera was rolling, but they couldn't hold back their cheers. It made Ethan smile. The day wasn't wasted, after all. Only a moron would have screwed up that shot. As he joined them squinting into the playback screen, the discussion was already underway.

'I don't like it.' Simon pushed out his bottom lip like a baby about to have a tantrum. 'Let's go back to the hill.'

'Why? What's wrong with it?'

'It's not on-brand.'

'What the hell does that mean?'

'We're not looking for that sort of shot,' Simon said. 'Take your places back up the hill.'

'What do you mean it's not on-brand?' Ethan said. 'You haven't got a clue what you're doing. You're just making us look like idiots. No-one's going to care about us riding down a slope. The skaters here are bored stiff and they're the ones you're supposed to appeal to.'

'Thank you, I've listened, and heard you out, but it's not working. Just get back up the hill and into position. That's why we're paying you.'

Only the problem was, this wasn't the reason why Ethan was there. He was there because he had to be. There was no extra money in it for him. The only person there for the money was Elliott, who looked completely dejected at the thought of working with a bunch of imbeciles. Elliott began walking back up the hill, but Ethan couldn't make the same walk.

'Let's get this thing done!' Elliott flapped his arms against his hips and wondered what the holdup was.

The kids had had enough and were ready to leave. They knew nothing else was going to happen. Simon motioned Ethan to get back up the hill and then started flicking through his script for the later scenes. This was the *real* problem. It wasn't ending with the hill roll. They had a whole script to get through.

He couldn't do it.

'No.'

'What do you mean, no?' Simon tried to pull rank. 'Let's get on with it. We're losing the light.'

'No. I'm done. I've had enough.' Ethan pulled his elbow pads off and threw them at the director's feet. Suddenly he felt a whole lot better as the frustration at how ridiculous they were making him look drifted away. Now, he just wanted to go home.

'Where are you going?' Elliott came back down the hill after him.

'You can stay if you want, but I'm not.'

'Oh great. Thanks for that. It's alright for you. I can't leave. I need this.'

The director joined them with a slew of complaints and threats. 'You're not leaving. The contract says you're mine for the day. Get back up that hill and put your pads on. Let's get this done!'

Ethan took off that stupid orange shirt and put his hoodie back on.

'Right. Have it your way,' Simon said. 'It doesn't matter.' He shouted over to an assistant in their media van. 'Tanya! Tell Clive to join us. This one's being thrown off set.' The assistant went to the van and a young man, wearing pads and a purple helmet, appeared in the doorway holding a pristine supermarket skateboard by the trucks.

Clive had indeed signed on the dotted line before checking the details. He probably thought, *How hard can skateboarding be?*

Simon seemed happy with the switch and couldn't see any problems. 'Say hello to your new wing-man,' Simon said. Clive's cheek bones bulged against his helmet straps.

'Jesus Christ,' Elliott said. 'You're not seriously going to let this goon ride with me? Ethe, you can't leave me here?'

'Don't do it,' Ethan said. 'They're making you look like a fool.'

Elliott was in that midway mode of panic: say

nothing or tell the director to shove it. The decision wasn't easy, and crucial seconds ticked by, as he began the walk back up the hill, until his conscience kicked him. Ethan couldn't hear what was said. But Simon suddenly had a look of shock on his face.

'What's happening?' Little Mikey was the first of the grommets to ask what all the fuss was about.

'I think.' Ethan still wasn't one hundred per cent sure. 'No. Now I am. We've both just quit.'

Elliott drop-kicked his pads into the shrubs and grabbed his bag.

'Don't worry. Something else will come up.'

'For you, perhaps. Chunks of cash like this don't arrive for me in a hurry. It might be a long time before I get another chance.'

'I'll let you know if something comes up. There's usually plenty of stupid ideas kicking around.' It felt good to get him on-side again, but Elliott had other ideas.

'Whatever you touch turns to shit. You just lost me this gig and the one hundred and fifty which goes with it.'

That punch left him dead in his tracks. So much for friends helping each other out. Ethan wasn't accepting no, though. He wanted to do something. A board company was a great idea, and the town needed it. If all it took was five hundred, then maybe there was a way?

3
THERAPY

The Physiotherapy gym at West Ubley Hospital squeaked with training equipment straining under the weak joints of its patients. The mild scent of disinfectant masked the smell of their frisbee-shaped sweat patches. High on the wall, a TV played the News with subtitles. A therapist in a dark blue uniform helped an overweight fifties woman rolling around on a yoga ball. Nothing said Privacy like the wind-pose, trouser-trump of a senior citizen in a public place. Blame the yoga ball on a polished floor. They looked everywhere for sympathy for their aches and pains: *It's here, no, here; That hurt; I think I've had enough; Isn't it hot in here?* Their polyester friction and youthful burnt-tyre memories coughed a soft-tissue death. They were the type who'd collapse in a heap of broken bones if stepped on

Lego and bruised as if they'd been beaten in an armed robbery.

Hospitals hated Ethan and the feeling was mutual. They issued countdown timers the moment you checked in, and disorientated you just long enough to get sloppy, slide up to someone friendly, touch a surface, and blam! You've caught Blue-spot Knob Disease or some incurable brain virus from South Africa requiring a six-month quarantine and a case of bedsores.

No thanks.

Heston pushed hard into some leg weights. He'd been coming here regularly for private sessions since the car accident. Ethan felt it in his pay packet, but after all he'd put his brother through, it was least he could do. There was a time in the future when he hoped things would get easier, Heston might stand on a board, and they could roll together again. Then there was the guilt. Ethan hated that the most.

'I've been looking at this new place.' Heston leg-lifted five-kilos. 'There's something about it. I don't know if it's right for me.' After a few more repetitions he was done.

Ethan had seen the brochure photo of a bungalow with a well-kept front garden.

'The agent hasn't had many offers and he is pushing to get me inside. He knows I've got the cash.' Heston wiped his face with a towel. 'It's nice, loads of room, fresh paint, but it gives me a weird feeling.'

'Maybe it just needs a good party to put some atmosphere into it? What are the neighbours like?' The stereo in the previous place stress-tested them to the limit.

'I'm going to sit on it for a while. That agent will be pissed, but I don't care. His desperation is making it look ugly.'

The TV news flashed up more details on the story from the morning's chemical theft at Holston Distribution. Unlike many planned and efficient crimes, this one had none of that. It was more of a lunatic meat-head raid than an organised crime spree. CCTV caught it all. A masked gang sent a hired Hummer straight in through the side doors, then took two more rams until the doors gave way and they left it propped up on internal bollards like a drunk Transformer. The gang ransacked the place, found what they were looking for, and loaded everything into the back of a second vehicle.

Officer Harding appeared on the screen and claimed the men were not armed and the public should not be worried. The reporter asked what they took: Ink. Go figure. They didn't take the specialist spraying equipment worth hundreds of thousands; they didn't go for the plant machinery either, probably on account of its size and weight. The police had some *strong leads* and *weren't going to rest* until the culprits were found and *brought to justice*. Textbook media training.

Who'd go to all that effort steal inks?

The whole thing stank.

The reporter turned back to the camera, summarised the events, and handed back to the studio.

'What the hell was all that about?' Ethan said.

'Something more valuable than us or the police know.'

'Talking of idiots. You've heard I've got the cinema steps this week?'

The cinema steps were a low five-set with no run-up, chipped to death, and virtually unrideable. No-one bothered. The mechanic next door occasionally put in a planning application to buy the old building, but it always failed. Everyone had their fingers crossed it would go through one day and be flattened.

'I've got a feeling the muppets in research—present company excluded—are just picking random locations to give to me. Anyone who knows anything about skating wouldn't pick that spot. There's loads of better places on the list.'

'It doesn't matter,' Heston replied. 'Give them what they want. That's all you've got to do. It's not going to be your problem if the results aren't good. Just don't get fired.'

'So, I've got to be just crap enough to be taken

seriously, but if I'm too bad, they'll fire me. I can't win.'

'You can win: be average. It's not that hard.' Heston had done the maths and reminded his brother that if he could convince N27 to end his contract, he'll be out of the company with twenty-grand in his pocket and freedom. However, if he quit, he'd get nothing.

Ethan grumbled at the thought of it. There's no way that he could even consider the steps, as they sucked. He needed something else, another angle, another spot.

'Can they fire me if I deliver a different edit to the one they're expecting?' Ethan hadn't read the legalese and mumbo-jumbo of his contract but knew Heston had.

'You have to stick to the schedule,' Heston reminded him.

'You said I had to deliver an edit. I'm still going to do that, but will changing the location get me fired?'

'You did that last week and Christ knows how you managed to…' Heston trailed off as he remembered Royston Hives' weed business. 'Forget that.' Heston began his thought again. 'You'll probably get another disciplinary. Get enough of those and they'll have a good reason to sack you.'

'I'll take that risk.'

4

TOE THE LINE

Ethan had a plan to improve his ratings, get more attention on his edits, and raise his company value. It's impossible to fire someone who brings success to the party, and N27 needs it more than ever. If they've been the cause of his problems, then he'll just have to sidestep everyone until the path is clear.

'I know you just want me to toe-the-line, but I've got a better idea. I can't believe there isn't a way out of this mess. I'm going to get my ratings so high at N27, every other skate company is going to want me.'

'How are you going to do that?' Heston doubted him yet again.

Ethan bit his tongue. 'I've got this idea to put on a skate event for everyone and film that instead of skating the cinema steps. I'll get some music happening and use what's left of the budget for prize money.'

'N27 will never go for it.'

'I won't tell them. Let them think I'm doing the cinema steps. The edit won't be what they're expecting, but they can't sack me, right?'

'It's a bit simplistic.' Heston rolled the idea around as the therapist switched to the other hip joint. 'I guess it *could* work.'

'Exactly. I could do it at the DIY spot.'

'You think it'll need be that easy to get Ren, Chris, and Elliott to forgive you?" Heston winced as another stretch on his left leg got stuck on some scar tissue.

'Ren'll need some work, but the others will be fine. I've already spoken to Chris and I saw Elliott yesterday. He'll be good too.' He had an idea for payment on the gate to bump up the prize fund, which Heston seemed to be fine with. Though he held back on his other idea of fixing the comp so Elliott won. Usually, he would have just blurted it out, but something stopped him. Elliott wasn't discussing his board company plan yet, and Ethan wasn't exactly sure if he could raise enough money yet.

'You'll need to get permission from the council,' Heston said.

'No, I won't.' Then a basketball-sized feeling set in his gut. 'Will I?'

'You need permission to hold an event on public land and there's no guarantee you'll get it. You've got to play by their rules otherwise they'll shut it down.' Heston asked his physio if he could take a break.

It was as good a time as any to show Heston what he'd been working on. He dug into his bag for a wad of leaflets and handed one over.

'What's this?" Heston scanned it. *'DIY skate carnage. Come and compete for £1000 cash prize in the best trick comp. Music, party hard, and blast the afternoon away. Doors open on the 8th at 2 pm, comp kicks off at 3 pm - until late.'*

'It's not a cash prize!' Ethan examined one of the leaflets himself. 'Shit. I said a thousand pounds worth of prizes. Dixel screwed up.'

The physiotherapist reminded him that he was in a public place and to keep his language in check.

'Are you sure *she* screwed up?'

'I know what I said. How am I going to get a grand? I don't have time to reprint them.'

'Just tell everyone you made a mistake.'

'I didn't. Dixel did.'

'Does it matter? Here's a better idea: don't bother and do the cinema steps instead.'

'No. I'm doing this.'

'Then why bother asking me?' Heston flipped the leaflet over and back again. He then broke into a chuckle. 'I guess I'm impressed for once. I've spent long enough looking after you, it's good to see you thinking for yourself. And Dixel's done a good job. These look great.'

Ethan couldn't explode at Dixel. She'd murder him for the mistake. A whole evening was spent doing them as a favour and he *was* grateful. But a grand felt like an impossible amount. Maybe he could call up a local company for sponsorship? It had been so long since he'd tried.

'You think it'll work though?' Ethan asked.

'It's not impossible.'

'Not impossible. I like those odds.'

The therapist returned and got Heston to lie down so she could work on another joint.

'Do you really care about N27 enough to do an exceptional job though?'

'I can try. They can't sack me if I'm getting them loads of attention and attracting new investors.'

'I think you're forgetting something. You're about one disciplinary away from being sacked, and it's a twenty-grand gamble. So, why is this even a conversation? Another company might not make an offer for you, or a legal challenge might not release you from your contract. That'll mean no more edits and no more stoked kids.' Heston winced in pain as the therapist rotated his hip joint to its limits.

'I've got no other options. This is exactly what I need to get everyone on my side again. And if it doesn't work, I promise I'll try your approach next time.'

'There might not be a next time,' Heston said. 'So, the cinema set is dead?'

Ethan was up and ready to leave. 'Dead and buried.'

5

TRIPLE RAILS

There was a heavy session already going on outside the Hill Street supermarket handrails by the time Ethan arrived. That afternoon, shoppers were being antagonised by skaters weaving around trollies and pushchairs. Usually, the faces were all the same, but since the summer, and a new term of Uni, skating had blown up. Students from all over the country mixed with the locals. Locals who Ethan had been trying to avoid, and those who knew about the beef between Ren, Elliott, and Ethan initially gave him a wide berth. The younger kids grabbed a flyer, before returning to the safety of the supermarket wall.

Ricard took one. That happy butterfly couldn't offend anyone even if he tried. He hadn't heard a thing at N27.

'They don't know about it yet. So, please,' Ethan

hated pleading, 'you've got to keep this one quiet. Otherwise, you could ruin it…' A little bit of passive-aggressive guilt should nail the urge to talk shut.

'No problem.' Ricard nodded and passed another leaflet on whilst reading his own.

Chris bounced into the conversation like a puppy. 'This looks good.'

'Spread the word,' Ethan said. 'It needs to be packed. Skaters, spectators, media, doesn't matter to me.'

'A grand cash!' Chris said loud enough for everyone to hear.

Ethan crumbled a little inside and swallowed the reminder. Typical of everyone to focus on the error. 'I'm still working on that. There will be prizes though, but I've got to contact some companies and sort out them out.'

'Like who?'

'All the big brands,' Ethan lied.

'Sweet.' Chris couldn't believe that something so good was happening right on their doorstep. 'With those N27 connections, you'll have no trouble.'

'Exactly.' Ethan felt the presence of someone by his shoulder and guessed who it was.

'Peddling your corporate bullshit?' Ren snatched a flyer out of his hand.

'It's a comp. Everyone's invited and we'll have plenty of free shit to give out.'

'A grand in cash,' Chris said.

'I said, I'm still working on that.' His gut knotted again as the sum lightbulbed above the foreheads of everyone holding a leaflet.

'You're missing something,' Ren said. 'The bit which says N27 will own everything filmed and sell it on to some company at a massive profit.'

'It's not like that,' Ethan said. He then lowered his voice. 'It's not even N27 approved. I'm going alone on this one. Yes, there will be filming, but it'll be a fun day for all of us.'

Ren flipped the flyer over then turned it back again. The money hooked him, no-one could miss it, and the comp was attractive. The prize was probably going to end up going to him or Elliott. Ren hesitated. He wanted to screw it up into a ball and throw it back at him, just for show.

'Elliott is down for it.'

'Bullshit he is.'

'I spoke to him yesterday afternoon whilst on a job and cleared everything up. He's coming, I swear.' He couldn't care whether Ren believed him or not. He'd cracked their veneer of silence, just for a moment, and that was a win. 'Are you coming too? It would be cool to get everyone together and see Elliott go off. He'll probably win it.'

'Who says that?' Ren said.

'I'm just saying. It's likely, that's all.'

Ren still couldn't figure out whether Ethan was

lying about Elliott approving. And now other skaters were listening in it was surprising that something hadn't already kicked off. Ren loved the drama of a good show and Ethan had nothing to lose. The flyer in Ren's hands must have flipped enough times to get dizzy before Ethan got bored waiting for a response and handed a few more out to the people around him.

'Just make sure there are no shitty N27 boards in the prizes.' Ren folded his flyer and put in his back pocket.

6

BOROCCA BOAT

Ethan spent the next couple of hours distributing leaflets to every skate spot and hang-out he could. Shoving them through letterboxes and giving them to anyone who'd take them. His small bundle slowly got lighter until, empty-handed, with aching feet, he knew he was done.

On the quiet canal path walk home, a tall, slim, well-dressed man, with a briefcase in one hand and a carrier bag in the other, stumbled beside a boat. He was balancing on one leg to get a footing aboard, and it wasn't working.

'Don't just stand there.' The man spoke loud and clear as if his ears were blocked. 'Take this case, will you?'

Balance was the main problem. He was drunk. It didn't matter how many steady hands and stable legs he engaged, none of them worked in the correct order.

The black leather suitcase looked expensive and important, and as the man was preoccupied, Ethan pushed the buttons. The latches popped open. There couldn't be anything valuable inside an unlocked case. He flipped the lid and saw stacks of stapled papers, two silver pens slotted in holders, and a fat diary-looking thing. Business cards said, *Dominic Borocca: Lawyer*. A file had a photo of a mid-forties man with slicked-back hair, shaved at the sides, and a distinctive tribal neck tattoo of concentric circles. The name underneath: A.D Boston. He looked like someone who had access to a range of car stereos.

'That is a very dangerous man.' The bony finger of Dominic Borocca tapped on the portrait. He didn't seem to care that Ethan had broken into his case. 'I'd have him behind bars if it wasn't for the barrister, Sampson.' Borocca stumbled back to the canal boat and tried again.

A white DIY Centre bag with something heavy inside bashed into his shins and made him howl. After enough failed attempts to get on the boat, Borocca chose to sit on the canal path grass. He took a small silver hipflask from his coat pocket and gulped an inch of it.

'That's a nice boat,' Ethan said.

'Really? I think it's pretentious; a symbol of left-wing gratuity; an eco-living mask whilst perpetuating the environmental myth.'

'Whatever the hell that means.'

'It means, we all exist in a broken system, chasing our own personal fix, and it's relentless and material, yet infinitely futile because no matter what we do—good or bad—we run a fatalistic path of complete self-destruction. Do you see what I'm saying?'

Ethan didn't, but gathered it was something to do with a broken system. 'The company I work for has been trying to screw me over since day one.'

Borocca asked the name of it and realised he'd heard of N27 before. 'Does the name, Michael Blacker ring any bells?' Ethan nodded. 'That man has a questionable back catalogue of shareholder dealings. Corporate fraud, I believe it was,' Borocca took another swig from the flask, 'which, I imagine, has followed him straight to the boardroom of your company.'

Ethan hadn't heard anything but took a note to remember the phrase *corporate fraud*. It sounded useful.

'They needed enough super-injunctions to line a kitty-litter tray to keep that one quiet,' Borocca added.

'So, you're a lawyer then?'

'I was, until a few hours ago.' Borocca told him that he'd been disbarred due to a minor incident with Jacob Sampson in the courtroom. 'Fifteen years of training and my livelihood gone for one little slap across a leathery jawline. Murderers receive less than that.' He pondered the moment as if replaying his final hour. 'I needed the break anyway. So, today is my last day on this earth. I know I'm not dying exactly, but in six months I'll be reborn, with a clean liver.'

'You're having surgery?'

'No. Therapy. Across the road there.' He pointed to what looked like a fancy B&B.

'Because of your drinking problem?'

'I suppose. But you don't need a problem to get in there. You just need a functional credit card number and expiry date.'

Borocca was adamant that he would get on the boat this time. He screwed the hip-flask lid on tight and put it back in his jacket, then picked up his bag, and began his tiptoe stretching game once more. Sooner or later, he was going to slip into that water.

'Before you drown yourself: do you know how I could get council permission to hold a public event at short notice? I've left it too late for the official route.'

The man heard but didn't reply. He was just mumbling swear words from the sixteenth century like a vexed ignoramus.

Ethan grabbed the boat's boarding plank and positioned it under Borocca's foot as he stabilised himself. He seemed mystified how this magical pathway appeared so perfectly for him and, with a euphoric smile, stepped on board.

'So, what's going to happen to your boat whilst you're away?' Maybe Borocca's partner would live there or get it moored elsewhere.

Borocca knelt and lifted a tin of paint from the plastic bag. He used a screwdriver to pop the lid off. 'Oh, this isn't mine. It belongs to Jacob Sampson.' He swung great globs of white over the decking and door. Huge thick splashes covered the dark wood flooring like cake icing. When the last dribble had left the tin, his drunken fog lifted. He slapped the paint covered screwdriver into Ethan's hand and walked off towards the retreat.

Then he turned as if he had forgotten something. 'Oh, and don't trust that N27 company.' He gave Ethan a little black voice recorder from his pocket. 'This will record continually for twenty-four hours. You never know when you'll need it.'

'I don't need it,' Ethan said. He had a phone which would do the same job.

'You never know when you'll need it!' Borocca repeated as he walked across the road. 'And don't tell the council about your little bloody party. The less they know, the better. Forgiveness is easier to get than permission.' He climbed the clinic steps and disappeared inside.

7

LINES. FOR. DAYS

The following day Ethan and Dixel paid a visit to the DIY spot built between two disused buildings. For ten years the skaters enjoyed sessions without any interruption, other than the occasional afternoon dog walker. No-one seemed to care about it and the developer had no intention of demolishing it without a massive Government brownfield incentive. Along the back lane was a secret rusty door, hidden behind an Ivy-covered wall. When given a hard kick, it popped free and stubbornly creaked open with a shoulder push. The area inside was covered in graffiti and about the size of an Olympic swimming pool.

'Oh, wow!' Dixel said. 'How have I not known this was here?'

'That moves by the way,' Ethan pointed at an

old lorry trailer at the far end. 'We've winched it aside with a 4x4 once to get a concrete mixer in.'

Banks and hips with crude coping lips. Blocks and ledges with wax-blackened edges. The sides had obstacles added each year, including a brutal wall-ride corner that everyone feared. A ghetto driveway with a flat bank hip. A kicker set front which everyone hit. Curb-stone hubbas, regular or switch. A four-set handrail that nobody missed.

Ethan went for a quick roll, getting some height on the transitions and looping back towards Dixel to carve over the little clamshell on the floor.

'We've got good light and it's pretty quiet, so let's get some filming done.' Dixel put her bag on the floor and started unpacking.

The filming started with Ethan powering across the driveway, straight up the wall ride, carving over a bricked-up window, then back down towards the driveway and ollieing over the whole thing. He almost slid-out on a tight left carve and scraped the rust off an eighteen-inch-high ledge with a short fast 50-50. A couple of pushes gave him enough speed for the corner wall-ride, then over the pump-bump nipple, to finish with a kickflip-indie over the volcano. He rolled away to the sound of his wheels crackling on tiny stones and broken concrete fragments.

Lines. For. Days.

Dixel switched out her flat lens for a fisheye and

sat in the corner wall-ride pocket. Ethan dropped in on the quarter and blasted up past her. He leant back and power-slid the vert section on the way back down.

The footage was great and continued. Even the stills she took were good enough for a front-cover. Full colour, staple-free, and poster-sized. Ethan came to a halt, out of breath, and took in some water. The next line needed some thought. Whilst a quick watch of the footage showed wheels screeching, bearings hissing, and the echo of ollie cracks and tail smacks.

An almighty explosion rippled the air around them and thudded his chest.

The blast and shock forced them to instinctively duck and cover. Starlings took to the sky and dogs barked in the distance. A plume of light grey smoke floated up from one of the nearby garages.

'What the hell was that?' Ethan said. 'A gas canister?' Then there was a worrying thought that someone could have been caught up in it.

'I'm going to look.' Ethan ran across the spot and out through the secret door. Dixel stuffed her camera in the bag and ran after him. After a hundred yards along the back lane, they reached the garages and immediately found the one they needed. The door was half open and had smoke still billowing out of it. Ethan heaved the buckled door up a couple of feet until it jammed in its runners. Inside was a huge room which had been converted into a makeshift lab. It was much bigger than the garage appeared from the outside. In the middle of the floor underneath a toppled shelving rack, plastic storage containers, and ventilation pipes lay the body of a dust-covered man in a lab coat. They lifted everything off as he groaned into consciousness. Dixel removed the chin strap of his facemask.

'Are you okay?'

The man coughed and spluttered and leant on his side to cough some more. Thick black rubber gloves were pulled off and slapped on the floor. He sat up, dazed and blinking. The name badge on his lab coat said, Joseph Priestley, senior lab technician - Zavier Labs Ltd. A pungent smell filled the room which irritated the nose and made Ethan spit.

'What are you doing here?' Priestley said. Ethan frowned at Dixel, both confused at his reaction. 'Who are you?'

Concussion

Dixel ignored his questions 'Are you okay? We heard the explosion and found you. What happened?'

Priestley coughed and got to his feet. 'None of your business.' He was in his late fifties, greying hair, and small wire-rimmed glasses. 'This is private property.'

It was hard not to become tetchy with a man

who had zero thanks to give. Other than a hole in the roof and crap on the floor, the lab didn't appear to have any other damage. The more he insisted their Samaritan efforts were wasted, the more Ethan wanted to stay and nose around.

'What are *you* doing here?' Ethan said sternly. 'These garages are residential, and this looks industrial.' He picked up a glass beaker, spun the liquid inside into a vortex, and recoiled at the odd smell coming from it.

8

ALLEY SPOT

'As I said, this is none of your business.' Priestley took the beaker from him and put it back on the desk. 'This is my lab. You're on my property and all of it is private.'

'It might be your lab, but it's about as private as a massive explosion. It wouldn't surprise me if the fire brigade and police are on their way over now.' Priestley knew Ethan was right. The explosion would have created a huge neon signpost pointing to the garages for the curious and the concerned to explore. 'You better get used to people being around here. By this time tomorrow, you'll have over a hundred people skating and spectating.'

Priestley lowered his voice and spoke slowly. 'I don't think *you* understand.' He sounded like a patronising supply teacher. 'You shouldn't be here today, tomorrow or ever. So, whatever you're planning, I suggest you cancel it.'

'I recognise this chemical name.' Dixel was at the back of the lab looking around the stock.

'Merely a B in GCSE Chemistry,' Priestley said. 'No? Then please tell me more…'

'Oh, patronising. Clever,' Dixel quipped. 'My mother works at Zavier Labs too.'

The chemist turned away from them and brushed his hands on his lab coat. When he turned back around Ethan noticed his name badge was missing. The guy was shifty as hell and about as legit as a fifty-quid complete setup. Ethan felt for the voice recorder which Borocca gave him. *Record everything. You never know when you're going to need it.* He powered it up, hit record, and placed it on the shelf near him.

Priestley went to the garage door and pulled it down. Clinical daylight bulbs blinked on and lit the entire lab space. About six garages had been knocked into one. Towards the back of the lab were pallets of boxes looking like they'd just arrived or were ready to leave. An eerie feeling hit him that they'd stumbled upon a Uni-bomber or something. Priestley went back to his lab bench, poured a couple of fluids together, and began mixing them.

'Let's see how good your chemistry knowledge is.' He held a small vial of silvery liquid. 'Do know what this is? Of course, you don't. This is an electrolyte. Did you know that LM alloy can be manipulated in ways not possible with conventional electrolytes? We can produce an effect called Electro-Wetting. LM can be exploited to coalesce and separate droplets under low voltages.'

'LM?'

'Liquid Metal electrochemistry.' Priestley seemed annoyed at Ethan's interruption. 'You've watched Terminator 2 Judgement Day, surely? With this approach to droplet interaction, we have a theory which accounts for oxidation-reduction as well as fluid instabilities based on simulations and experimental analysis. This...' He jiggled the fluid in the container. '... allows separation which arises in bipolar electrochemical reactions, which leads to interfacial tension. So, the liquid metal is used to create a field-programmable electrical switch.'

'The only thing I understood there, was "switch",' Ethan said.

Priestley poured another liquid out of a container. 'And, as with conventional relays, the system can transition between bio-stable separate states, which makes it useful for shape programmable circuitry.'

'And that means what?'

Priestley held out a tub of clear liquid for Ethan to take. Once his hands were free, he put on a face mask and thick gloves. Whatever was in that tub, stank.

Dixel realised where she had seen these chemicals before. They were mentioned in the news report from the Ink theft. She took a photograph of the label with her phone.

'Keep very still,' Priestley said. He put a heavy apron on and what looked like a welder's mask. He then placed two electrodes into the fluid and attached both cables to a little box on the workbench.

'You're holding a very rudimental liquid metal switch in a very unstable chemical. The low voltage is keeping the droplets apart. Stop the charge or…' Priestley searched for the right word, '… move too much. And. Boom!'

Ethan wanted to fling that container across the room, but he had just seen an explosion almost take the ceiling off a building. He didn't move. He couldn't move, let alone take his eyes off the fluid level. His feet were stuck, but his brain was speeding at a hundred miles per hour.

His hands shook.

The liquid began to ripple.

9

DIXEL'S MUM

'I'll ask you again: Cancel any plans you have for an event, and stay away from this area today, tomorrow, and forever. The alternative is in your hands. If you want to keep them, that is.'

'You're going to blow us up?!' Dixel shouted at him. 'What kind of crazy are you?'

'Yes,' Priestley said flatly. 'The same fluid you're holding is in multiple containers around the room,' He pointed to three forty-five-gallon drums. 'Above them are ventilation shafts which will ensure the blast is carried to every corner of the lab within a tenth of a second. Everything will be destroyed beyond any recoverable recognition. Neat, don't you think? It's like the system built into ejector seats, with enough power to launch a man sixty metres in the air.'

Ethan tried to breathe slowly. He was getting

hot too. That liquid wouldn't stop wobbling no matter how much he tried to hold it steady. Priestley was either bullshitting or crazy, but whichever it was, he wanted out of there and so did Dixel.

'Okay, of course. We won't be back. Now can you take this off me?'

'Good.' Priestley took the electrodes out of the fluid and set them on the bench, then slowly lifted the tub from his hands. The moment Priestley opened the garage door, Ethan and Dixel got out of there as fast as they could.

The following morning, Ethan was sitting on a curb, waiting for Dixel's mum to pick him up and drive them over to the DIY spot. Dixel had tried to get him to cancel it in a shitty text-message exchange, but he couldn't, not just yet. He needed more time to think. A restless night of interrupted sleep didn't help. Whenever he felt tired and shut his eyes, his mind wouldn't settle. And when he did eventually sleep, he dreamt about Priestley in the garage.

A silver Saab pulled up against the curb.

Priestley wouldn't blow the place up. How could a man go from dumb shed-chemistry—and personal endangerment, at most—to killing kids? It didn't add up. He must be all threat and no action.

Dixel shouted at him to get in.

Ethan refocused on the figure hanging out of the passenger-side window waving at him. He grabbed his bag and board and jumped in the back. The car was clean and the seats were hard as if nobody ever sat on them. The local radio was on in the background.

Dixel's mum was driving. 'Pleased to meet you.' She was smartly dressed and had a black cord neckless with a silver circular pendant hanging from it. She had a friendly soft motherly face.

'Thanks for the lift, Mrs Manning.'

'Neela, please. And it's no problem.'

'So, as I was saying,' Dixel interrupted. 'Can you remember the name of that guy in the garage?'

'Joseph Priestley. Why?'

'That's him!' Dixel said. 'Do you know him?' Her mum thought for a moment then shook her head. 'Can you look him up?'

'It's a big company with a lot of departments,' Neela said. 'He might not even be in the UK division.'

'Can you talk to your boss? I don't know. Do something.'

'And say what? *One of our employees is connected to the chemical theft?*'

Dixel looked puzzled. 'Yes, Mum. Jesus. Why is that so hard?'

'Because it sounds ridiculous, which will then

make me look ridiculous. You can't just accuse people of things. You need evidence.'

'Aren't two witnesses enough?'

'Besides, I'm working on a sensitive project at the moment … Leave it with me.'

'My god. Grow a spine. I know the company is full of old white men, but it's not the eighties. People will take you seriously.'

'I said, leave it with me. I'll look into it.'

'Oh, yeah. Totally not important as you drive your child into the hands of a terrorist.'

The conversation stopped as the entrance to Tenison road was blocked by a barrier. Neela pulled up alongside the vehicle and asked what the problem was. They were from the Environment Agency and a fifties woman with a hard expressionless face stepped up to the window.

'Sorry, but the road has been closed off due to a chemical leak. The area is unsafe. You'll have to turn around.' The woman stepped back from the car as if the conversation was over, but Dixel's mum was having none of it.

'What sort of chemical exactly and what quantities?' The EA officer didn't reply straight away. 'I can't give any more details until we have the toxicity report back. Please turn the vehicle around. The road should be open again within 24 hours.'

'24 hours?' Neela looked back into the car and rolled her eyes. 'This is ridiculous.' She wasn't done with the officer. 'What are the contamination levels and how big is the cordoned perimeter?'

A male EA officer came up to the window. 'Turn the car around, please. This is not a conversation.'

'Fine,' Neela said. 'If you can't even tell me the radius of the quarantine, I'll just go to the other end of the road and get to my office that way.' She put the car in reverse, accelerated back quickly and put the steering wheel on a full lock like a racing driver. 'I've dealt with enough chemical incidents in my time and this doesn't resemble any of them.'

'Slow down,' Dixel said. 'It's not the end of the world.'

'I'm not cancelling the event…,' Ethan said.

'Shut up about your dumb event.'

Neela pulled out onto the main road. 'I can prove the area is safe in ten minutes. We've got a multi-million-pound sensor system built into the building which would have picked up any suspicious compounds in the air and alerted our emergency team.'

Neela stopped in a Zavier Labs parking bay and checked her phone for emails. 'Nothing's been reported. Those officers won't find anything.'

'You're sure it's safe?' Dixel said.

'Of course,' her mum stressed. 'I can't be so sure about your back garden chemist, but the air is clean. Either way, keep your phone on.'

'Of course, I will.' Dixel remembered photographing the chemical label from Priestley's lab and showed her.

'Where did you take this?' She studied the photo.

'From his lab.'

'It's a completely non-toxic, specialist ink, but not dangerous, at all.'

'Does it smell like something's died?' Ethan asked.

'It does, but it's not worth closing a road over.' Neela handed back the phone and said she had to get into work.

'That's good enough for me. The event is on. I knew he was a joke.'

'That explosion wasn't a joke.'

It wasn't until Ethan and Dixel were half-way across the car park that he remembered about the voice recorder. 'I left it running. If Priestley's got anything to do with the chemical theft and mentioned it in the Lab, it'll be on it.' Borocca told him it was only good for twenty-four hours before overwriting itself. It was already late morning which meant he only had a few hours left.

There wasn't anything they could do for the time being as people would be arriving soon. Dixel wondered how many people would actually turn up, but Ethan didn't care as long as the right people did. He knew Ren and Elliott wouldn't be able to resist that grand cash prize.

He decided not to mention her printing error.

Dixel was still worried about Priestley. For her, it was simple: change the date, get the police in, and hold an event afterwards. But Ethan feared the DIY spot could disappear overnight with all that fuss. He didn't want to tell anyone and was certain that everything would be fine. It was just a skate and some fun times. Bring in the police and they'd shut it down, putting it all over the news so fast they'd never skate there again. There was no question of cancelling as far as he was concerned. Dixel's mum was sure the chemical was non-toxic and he trusted her more than those EA officers. Besides, the further away they got from the garage the less it smelt, anyway.

'He might be a nutter,' Ethan said. 'But I think he's harmless as long as we stay away from him. What's he going to do when there's a hundred people packed in here?'

10

DO NOT CROSS

By the time Ethan and Dixel got to the DIY spot entrance, people were already crowding around the barrier hassling the Environmental Agency officers to get in. He didn't recognise any faces yet but was stoked his promotion had worked. The closer they got, the louder and more frustrated the voices became. The officers wanted everyone to move back and repeated they wouldn't be allowed access. No-one left. Only a couple of plastic A-frame barriers and some *Do Not Cross* tape flapping in the breeze prevented two dozen people from pushing through. The officers' patience was being tested. Something was going to crack. It was just a matter of time.

Dixel's mum called. She said she would if she found something out. Ethan hoped it wasn't bad news. She had looked up the chemical and confirmed it could act as a fluid-switch if an electrical current was applied. Dixel played it down.

'I'm just asking,' Dixel said. 'He didn't say he would. No mum, nothing's going to happen. We're all safe and the Environmental officers are dealing with everything. We're fine.' Her mum's worry clattered through that phone call like marbles in a washing machine. Dixel repeated, *Fine*, many more times before finally hanging up. 'We've got a problem. Priestley was right. With enough current and the right mixture, the fluid is combustible.'

'How powerful? Deadly, or just removing my eyebrows?'

'There were three forty-five-gallon drums of the stuff, remember? What do you think?'

'It still doesn't make sense. Why would he do it?'

'Does it matter? He told us what he would do and we saw the blast.'

'That Lab must have thousands of pounds worth of equipment in there. Why blow everything up? Everyone's got to have a reason to do something.'

'Psychos don't.'

'But even psychos *think* they're smart. Blowing themselves up isn't smart. I don't think we should cancel. The EA officers are all over it. Sooner or later they'll discover the source of the chemical and deal with it. Then Priestley will be their problem, not ours.'

'You want to take that chance?'

'We're no threat to him. We don't care what he's doing back there. It's nothing to do with us. He's bluffing'

'And if he's not?'

'Then.' Ethan thought quickly and even surprised himself how much his usual dumb ideas weren't sneaking through. 'I'll get the voice recorder from the garage and listen to the recording. If there's any worry, anything at all, I'll pull the plug. How's that sound?'

It was the best solution they had between them and eventually, Dixel agreed too. And with the decision made, now all they had to do was get past the EA officers.

'Can you hang onto my board?' Ethan looked beyond the crowd. He'd seen something.

Dixel didn't have a chance to refuse. 'Where are you going?'

'How are they going to get everyone out if we're already inside skating?' He pushed his way through the crowd and along the side of the building. A set of bins allowed him to get up onto the wall and scamper across the flat roof. He climbed the fire escape steps to a second level and ran across to another wall. The EA officers were now out of sight, but he could still see their barrier. A blue transit van pulled up in the car park which he recognised. It was one of Bryon Dunkley's friends, Steve, with the sound system. Ethan ran to the wall nearest the car park and whistled down.

11

TWO LITTLE DUCKS

'Steve! Up here. On the roof.' Steve eventually spotted him. 'The entrance is blocked. I'll explain later. Swing the van around the back or you won't get in.' Steve put his thumb up and reversed out of the road. Ethan went to the far side and dropped down a level. A white minibus drove in and pulled up alongside the transit. Probably more skaters. They spoke for a moment and Steve waved his hand back towards the entrance. They pulled away again with the minibus completing a U-turn to join Steve on the main road.

Ethan made his way all along the first-floor roof edge, looking for a suitable spot to drop. When he reached a section with a window ledge below, he used it to lower himself down. In the back lane, everything was quiet: no cars or people. He followed the fencing line around the corner and heard Steve's van chugging down the lane. Ethan reached to the hidden door but found a fresh padlock on it.

Priestley.

Steve's van pulled up alongside and he wound down the window.

'Have you got any tools?' Ethan asked. 'I need bolt croppers or a hammer.'

Steve lifted a crowbar from the passenger footwell. 'Try this.'

Ethan jammed the small end into the eye of the lock and wedged the point into the brick mortar. He leant his body weight onto the lever and broke the lock open with ease. Nothing was going to stop him from getting this session underway. No EA officers. No crazy chemist. And certainly no dumb padlock

The skaters climbed out of the minibus, buzzing at the thought of a session when everyone else was stuck at the front of the building. They followed Ethan through to the spot, and as soon as footsteps hit the ground, the sound of wheels followed.

Ethan and Steve carried a pair of speakers in and put them on window ledges. Steve went back and grabbed the amplifier whilst Ethan fed the power cable through a broken window. Someone had smashed open the mains box years ago and reconnected the power supply. No-one ever expected it to stay connected, but so far, no-one seemed to care or noticed the extra on their monthly payments. Within minutes, Steve had the speakers connected to his mixer and laptop and turned up the volume on a playlist.

A breakbeat thumped out, echoing off the walls and summoning the rest of the riders. Something was happening inside and they weren't included. The already restless visitors got even more agitated. Any excuse used by the goons on the gate to hold people back crumbled like the brickwork. The moment someone hopped the barrier the rest rapidly followed. The EA officers couldn't do anything to stop them. With the barrier breached, even the spectators casually walked past the officers, empathising over their lost fight.

The session didn't need much planning. People knew the deal. Within minutes it was rammed with chaotic fun and a death-match of collisions which entertained the crowd. Steve announced there would be thirty minutes of open skating before a jam session of four people at a time. Anybody wanting to ride needed to stump up five quid and register.

Ethan sat back on an oil drum and watched the session grow. These were his people, at last. And even though no-one had spoken to him yet, it was like the old crew were back again. For the briefest moment, he imagined a conversation with someone at N27 and the bullshit he'd have to go through explaining everything to morons who couldn't understand how important this event was. Whatever they'd throw at him, it would be worth it. He pushed it out of his mind and remembered the voice recorder. He didn't really care for it, and Dixel wouldn't know if he listened to it, but he had to at least try. There was still a chance Priestley might do something stupid after all.

He slipped out through the back door again and into the lane. The minibus was an immaculate new hire, but inside it was devastation. The seats were covered in fast food packets—they had driven a long way. On the floor, a socket-set wrench, a snapped deck, and old shoes. The back doors had brand new stickers: Independent, Palace, and Supreme.

As Ethan reached the end of the lane and the start of the garages, he cautiously peered around the wall to check it was clear. Priestley's was number twenty-two. Two little ducks. The garage door was shut and he had no plan to find out if it was unlocked. Priestley might have electrocuted the handle for all he knew. Instead, he counted the number of doors then went through the back gate along the path that lined the back of the resident's gardens. He counted six garages up on the right and as he got close, operatic music could be heard from inside.

He tried the door.

It opened and he stepped inside.

The floor to ceiling shelving racks and boxes meant he couldn't see Priestley. Big white tubs of what looked like chemicals were stacked up to head height and provided perfect cover. The voice recorder was still where he left it, tucked away on a shelf almost twenty-four hours ago. If it wasn't turned off soon, it would start to overwrite itself. Suddenly, the music stopped and a ringtone echoed. Ethan ducked behind a pallet as Priestley stood to retrieve the phone. The sound of music from the event hummed from outside. Priestley's call quickly became heated with whoever was on the other end.

In a furious rant he commanded, 'Get everyone out at all costs. If you don't, I will.'

12

EA BLOCKED

Priestley was more deranged than Ethan thought. He was up on his feet pacing around. Whatever his plan was, the call made it sound like it was quickly slipping through his fingers. Ethan noticed those drums containing the chemicals and had to think fast to ruin Priestley's clean-up plan. Destroying the lab was one thing, but risking everyone else's life was another. That voice recorder would have to wait. Every time he looked at those barrels of fluid, he pictured himself shaking with the small tub in his hands. He couldn't move them without disturbing the contents. They'd blow for sure, and if one went, the rest might. Maybe if he blocked them instead?

Priestley opened the garage door and stepped outside to continue his call.

A pallet behind Ethan looked easier to move

than a huge barrel. He got on the floor and pushed it with his feet, inch by inch, closer towards the barrel. Each push scraped a nail across the floor and let out a screech from the cement. Priestley couldn't hear anything with the event music in the air and his focus on the call. After a few pushes, Ethan managed to get it to almost touch against the drum. That was far enough. He couldn't risk touching it. Next, he pulled the ventilation shaft to one side and hooked it behind a rack of shelving. Now the blast would spread around the room and not where Priestley wanted it. It would have to do. Ethan saw something familiar trapped between the packages of the pallet's contents, but he couldn't quite make it out. He turned on his phone torch and looked closer at what looked like a leaflet.

Then the design became clear. It was a twenty-pound note.

Ethan tore into the packing and pulled it out. A lucky find, or so he thought until he looked deeper. *There might be more*. He ripped open the hole in the paper packing and pinched several sheets and wiggled them out. He fanned through them and took a guess it was a grand's worth. The pallet was stacked with money-bricks of hundreds of thousands of pounds, maybe more. Without thinking, he split the money and stuffed it in his front pockets. That was enough. He didn't need anymore.

He didn't *need* any more.

But…

He tore into the packing paper and checked how Priestley was doing. He was still outside on his phone. Ethan removed one complete bundle and felt the weight of it. The density mesmerised him for a moment. There was more than enough cash, more than he could count, and enough to solve a lot of problems for a long time.

A brown fuzzy lump scampered across the floor and startled him. Before he'd registered it was a rat, he'd already bumped into the shelving behind him. It was only a gentle knock, but they weren't secured, and multiple heavy rolls of steel tubing began rolling slowly forward. He couldn't stop them. Everything happened slowly, unbelievably, and inevitably as they landed in a deafening clank and clatter of metal on the floor.

Shit. Ethan scurried away on all fours to the far side of the room behind some boxes. Priestley came in and kicked the tubing back, almost unsurprised that it had fallen. The re-stacking could wait, that call was more important.

'I'm waiting for the collection now,' Priestley said. 'Get through the crowd and use some initiative. We need to get this exchange completed.' He moved back out of the garage again.

Priestley must have people out in the event, mixing with all the spectators. Ethan knew he had to leave. He'd done his best, it was time to get out of there, let someone else deal with the lunatics. He grabbed his bag, collected the voice recorder, stuffed the money in his bag and left through the back door. His breath was short, and his thoughts were laser focused. The job was done. He couldn't believe he had so much cash and the recorder.

On the way out he almost collided with a short stocky dark-haired guy blocking his path. It could have been one of Priestley's gangs who had seen him climb down off the roof.

'Where are you going?' the man said. His arms wide, preventing Ethan from passing. All he could think about was the money in his bag. He was caught red-handed. Questions raced around in his mind: Who was he? How much had he seen? Did he know about the pallet move? Ethan didn't know what to say, he just glanced left and right looking for a way out. As soon as he moved the man grabbed his wrist and twisted it behind his back. The pain forced him to the floor within a second. He got an arm loose and tried to flip over, but it was useless. With the weight of the man on top, all he could do was snatch at the loose fabric of his clothing. He tried to head-butt the man but couldn't connect. The fight was fast, scrappy, and quiet, yet he couldn't get in control. Every move was counteracted until he ran out of energy and stopped struggling.

'What do you want? Get off me!' Ethan tried

not to shout in case Priestley heard, and he didn't know who was the greater threat.

'I'll ask the questions,' the man said. He dropped a knee on Ethan's legs to prevent any kicks. Ethan managed to get a hand free and picked up a half-house-brick.

It landed, hard.

The man went limp and slumped to the floor.

He pushed the man off and got up. One of Priestley's goons, no doubt. He deserved to get lumped. Blood appeared from the side of man's head. He'd never whacked someone like that before and didn't know what damage he'd done. He felt for a pulse and was relieved to find the man was just unconscious.

The side of the man's jacket slipped open and exposed the handle of a modern black pistol tucked in his waistband. Ethan froze. He hadn't been around guns enough to know anything about them, but it certainly didn't look like an airgun. It was real. There was no way he was getting shot for the sake of some money or that chemist. Ethan scooped up his bag, ran to the end of the path, vaulted over the gate, and got into the lane without looking back.

13

SENSORY OVERLOAD

Ethan followed the sound of the music back towards the packed skate spot. Steve attempted to shout out the names of tricks he didn't know. The skaters found it hilarious and the spectators didn't know any better. Ethan's mind was shot with twitchy thoughts and felt distant from the whole thing. People he knew nodded and said *Hi* as he passed, but they didn't know what was going on just a dozen metres away. The right thing to do would be to jump on the mic and tell everyone, or shut up and blend in, or eject and run with all the weight of that cash on his back.

Steve removed his headphones from one ear. 'Where've you been? Take the mic. I've got to go to the van.'

'I can't, sorry.' Ethan filtered back into the

crowd with his head down to avoid conversations. Steve shouted after him, but the noise soon took over. It was safer in amongst everyone, but he didn't know who to trust. The skaters, he could handle, but there were so many spectators, and any one of them could be from Priestley's gang. This wasn't what he signed up for. He felt as though he was just a sniff away from what the police would call a *Situation* or an *Incident*. He wanted nothing to do with it.

Skaters cheered with all the wood and urethane clattering on concrete, and the crowds Ooo'd and Ahh'd with the bails and slams. The spot wasn't designed for bystanders, but people found their viewing points anywhere they could, on blocks, walls, and windowsills watching riders hit the handrail. He was missing the best trick comp and couldn't give a shit about it. That voice recorder was safe in his pocket. He held his board across his chest like a shield and gripped that rucksack shoulder strap as if letting go would kill him. No-one was following, he knew that, but it only took a few paces before he needed to check again.

Andy spotted him and was all smiles and praises. Chris slapped him on the back and thanked him for setting it up. He forced a smile so fake someone should have noticed. Andy pulled Elliott over by his shirt and told him who to thank for the day.

'I know.' That was all Elliott could manage before turning away, but Andy pulled him back. He was his old arrogant self again, and a big difference from that day filming and begging for work.

Ethan didn't care or have enough straight thinking to hate on anyone. Someone nudged him on the shoulder. It was Dixel holding a beer for him.

'Did you get it?' The most important thing in her world was that voice recorder. 'Have you listened to it yet?'

'I think we're way beyond that.'

'What do you mean?'

'I'll tell you later. I can't hear a thing here.' Ethan took the beer but didn't drink it.

'What's the matter with you? You look a bit edgy.'

What's with all the bloody questions? 'I've got to get to the police,' he said.

'Why? What happened? Are we safe?'

'Yes. No. I don't know.'

'What does that mean? Make your mind up, are we, or aren't we?'

Ethan gave her the beer, but thought again, grabbed it back and downed it. 'Damn. I needed that.'

Dixel tried another million questions, but Ethan's senses couldn't settle.

'Get out there and skate. Join your friends.' She grabbed his bag off his shoulder, but he snatched it back and left. 'What's the matter with you? Where are you going now?'

14

RELUCTANT HOLD

All he could think about was getting out of the event, away from the crowd, and finding someone who could help. He wasn't sure who, but it had to be someone of authority. Someone with the power to bust back into the garages and shut down Priestley. Preferably someone with a gun.

As the crowds thinned out, he saw an officer from the Environmental Agency by the barriers. They weren't the best bunch to deal with, but they would have to do. They had radios and cars, and could get assistance, quickly. Some skaters were heading into the event and wanted to know why he was leaving. The chit-chat had to wait.

The female EA officer didn't look pleased to see him. He carried a skateboard: the international symbol of mouthy timewasters. The male EA officer was trying to guide some late arrival spectators off the site, insisting the event was unauthorised. They weren't leaving easily, when they could see people ahead of them, obviously having fun. The female officer was carrying a little too much weight. She hoisted her shoulders up and puffed her chest out like an inflatable. The name tag on her jacket said, *Diane*.

'I've just seen this guy in one of the garages,' Ethan said.

Diane leant in close for listening.

'I think he created your chemical leak. We need to get the police here as soon as possible.'

'Tell me exactly what you've seen.' Diane slid her finger around her belt like it was pinching her muffin.

Ethan told of the chemist, his explosion, his threats, and how Dixel had seen the inks from the distribution centre robbery.

'So as soon as I realised this guy was nuts, I left this recorder running overnight.' Ethan showed her the device. Diane tried to take it from him, but he wasn't letting go of it quite yet.

'I'll pass it to the right people,' Diane said. 'Besides, if there's valuable information about the leak, we need to know about it.'

Ethan wasn't so sure. 'I'll hold on to it until then.'

'Until the police get here, technically, we are the

police.' Once Diane realised Ethan wasn't handing it over, she went and spoke to her colleague.

'You have some information about the chemical leak, is that true?' The officer's name tag said, *Bob* and he spoke close and quiet as if it was just between the three of them. Bob also had the gravity of a hangover, which made Ethan step back a little.

'Where are you going?' Bob grabbed Ethan's arm, but he shook it loose.

'I'm not going anywhere. Just give me some space, that's all.'

'We need you to wait here until the police arrive and then we can take a statement. Is that okay?'

It felt like a reasonable request. The problem with Authority was Procedure. The two went hand in hand and once that ball started rolling, stopping it was impossible.

'How about you wait here in the car for a minute?' Diane said. Bob opened the door.

'I'll wait here.'

'The police are only going to be a few minutes,' Bob insisted. 'Take a seat.'

15

NUTBAR

'No thanks.' Ethan glanced back towards the event. 'Get the police here.'

Diane got on her radio, at last. Finally, they were doing something. It took them long enough. He started to feel a bit more comfortable now he was away from that nutbar with the gun. At least he was with someone with authority, even if they were slow to act. He wondered how long all this was going to take. The police only needed to take his details, surely, and send someone over to the garages and check out his claims. They could interview him for as long as they wanted after Priestley was in cuffs. With any luck, he could get back to the event and skate before the whole thing was over. It was all wishful thinking because it probably wasn't going to happen. The more he thought about it, the more he figured he'd just lost the rest the day.

Diane was still on the call, and Bob lingered like a fart in a forty-inch jacket. His late afternoon shadow anchored him to the spot like his presence meant something. Diane kept looking over. The kind of look which said, *maybe*, *not sure*, *probably*, and *okay*.

More EA officers carried on with their work on the other side of the car park. It figured that all sorts of procedures snowballed once a chemical leak alarm went off, even if Dixel's mum was sure it was unnecessary. The team checked boxes and shifted them away in a van. It looked like they'd done it a million times before because they had the process dialled. A box came out, they'd go through it, mark it off on a clipboard, and before it was packed in the van, another was ready for checking. It looked like the ultimate dull job. They only had a four-man team with a thousand boxes to go through.

Dummies.

One guy had trouble getting a stack of boxes on a sack truck and almost lost the lot over the floor. An easy mistake as the floor was crappy. Another guy took a knife and slid it up the packing paper around the boxes. The batch must have looked good as they loaded the lot into the van without checking. The next load had little white packages and appeared to be much lighter than the first.

Sack truck guy looked familiar. It wasn't until he

turned that Ethan noticed his tribal neck tattoo. The same design he'd seen in Dominic Borocca's briefcase. He tried to recollect what Borocca had said. Something about being dangerous and should have been in prison. They turned around the stack of boxes and examined the damaged corner. One of the men whistled over to Diane and she shuffled over like her shoes hurt. After they spoke for a moment. It was clear a package was missing.

Ethan gripped his backpack. He knew what they were looking at.

Diane's feet weren't hurting anymore on the walk back. Her polyester thighs zipped across that carpark.

The whole EA deal was bullshit. Dixel's mum was right. There was no chemical leak. Those people were working with Priestley. They were the gang.

He bolted.

Diane shouted at Bob, but Ethan was fifty paces ahead and running straight for the crowd. He didn't have to look around to know those officers were after him. They ploughed into the crowd, hassling people, flipping off hats, turning anyone around in a dark top, in the hunt for their man. Ethan kept pushing through the crowd as fast as he could, ducking and weaving and trying to make himself invisible. It would have been quicker to run through the skate session, but that would have exposed him.

Instead, he worked his way around the sides until he got to the back door. He slammed it shut and moved a dumped car tyre in front of it. It wouldn't hold them for long, but maybe just long enough.

He needed to get back up on the roof somehow. The gap between the minibus and the wall was too far apart to climb and jump across. There was no time to faff around stacking crates and boxes to get up there. He moved back along the lane trying to find a lucky foothold but was only forced further and further back. The officers broke out through the back door and must have radioed ahead as two more officers appeared at the end of the lane. Ethan's only route was through the garages and Priestley was already there to greet him. He suddenly felt like he was stuck in a Venus flytrap: struggling was futile; jaws slowly closing; certain death.

'I don't know what you're doing here, but I haven't seen anything,' Ethan pleaded. 'I'm not interested in the slightest. I've got a voice recorder with some information on, maybe, I don't know, but you can have it.' He held it up and expected someone to take it. 'Have it. I don't want it. Just let me leave.'

Priestley calmly walked towards him. 'I told you not to come back.'

16

A CASH EJECTION

'I don't want to cause any trouble and I'm sorry I hit your man out the back.'

'What man?' Priestley looked puzzled.

'The guy at the back of the garage with the gun. He stopped me as I left.'

Priestley had a little panic in his eyes. 'Shut the place down!' Two agents knew exactly what that meant and immediately went back out into the lane. 'Clean up everything. I don't want anything left behind.' Priestley went back into his lab and the remaining agents left the other way down the lane to the main road.

Ethan suddenly felt grateful that they were no longer interested in him. He didn't need a second telling to get out of there either. He made his way back into the event, but within seconds police sirens followed. Three cars appeared out of nowhere by the main entrance, as well as a riot van at the back as officers swarmed the buildings. Initially, the spectators hadn't realised with the music at full volume watching the skating. Ethan didn't know where to go or even whether to run at all. From one of the platforms, he saw the officer's cordon off the exit and guide people away. As more and more people realised the police had arrived, word spread through the session and, skaters being skaters, assumed they were after them. One of the police officers got out of the car with his gun drawn, and Ethan recognised the fresh cut on the side of his head. The officer ran around the back and went into the building. The moment only took a few seconds, but everyone noticed, and things suddenly got serious. The mood changed and now no-one resisted the orders to leave.

The police must have had the whole place under surveillance.

The chaos and confusion increased as more skaters realised the event was being shut down. Steve killed the music and an officer announced that everyone had to remain calm and move quickly to the old cattle market building. Officers waved people in the right direction, but despite this, some spectators decided to lop their heads off and run around in a chicken screaming panic.

Everyone was told to keep away from the windows, but no-one wanted to miss the show outside. The officer on the door couldn't do anything about it. The parents kept their kids far back, but everyone else fought for a good view.

And they got what they wanted.

A massive explosion popped and shook the floor.

The windows wobbled, but nothing smashed.

Ethan knew where it came from without even looking. He'd heard that sound before. A blur of papery smoke launched into the air. It took a moment to realise what it was. Redirecting Priestley's drum had jettisoned money into the sky like confetti. Hundreds of thousands of pounds in twenty-pound notes fell across the DIY spot. All the skaters initially laughed then quietened as they realised it was money.

The place went nuts.

Everyone pushed out through the police officer on the door and began scooping up cash like it was a snow day. Hundreds of pounds filled their pockets and as fast as they cleared the floor it rained even more. Happiness literally fell from the sky. People couldn't get enough of it.

There was no way Priestley and the gang could get their vehicles out. Police officers surrounded them in seconds. With no-where to go, the gang were trapped and surrendered immediately. Ethan watched it all unfold as he was probably the only person not interested in loading his pockets. The police had no interest in dealing with people grabbing the cash until all the gang were handcuffed. Then only the greedy and the desperate got caught. The smart people grabbed just enough to not make a scene and leave whilst the chaos was on. Everyone else stayed too long, grabbing every last sheet in a balance of justice for all the bad cards they'd been dealt. The police ended up collecting three bin-bags full of crumpled notes as people tried to leave. Even the good samaritans must have found it hard to hand back all that good fortune, though no-one got in any real trouble despite cautionary warnings blowing around like Rizla papers.

Ethan wasn't so lucky. The police had him marked from the moment they got there.

17

SHAKEN PRIORITY

Officer Harding's weighty hand landed on Ethan's shoulder as if he was the solution to all his problems. Ethan just wanted to get away, but that hand gripped him like molasses on a cat.

'A little bird told me that you've got some evidence.'

Ethan reached into his bag and pulled out the voice recorder. 'I've no idea what's on it, but it's yours.'

'I'll need to take a look at that camera,' Harding said to Dixel.

She powered up the camera and skipped back a dozen minutes and played a clip of several EA officers wheeling pallets in and out of a building.

'That's great.' Harding had seen enough and held out his hand.

'You're not taking my camera. This is mine. I'm using this.'

'It's evidence.'

'I get that, but you're not having it. I need this for work.'

Officer Harding gave a sympathetic tilt of his head.

'Don't patronise me.' Dixel switched off the camera and held it tight.

Harding sighed like his day was getting more difficult and he didn't have time to waste. 'I don't need the whole thing. All I need is a copy. You'll have to come with me to the station and transfer it.'

Dixel popped out the SD card and handed it over. 'I want that back.'

'Of course.' Harding took out a plastic bag from his jacket and dropped the card inside. 'As soon as we're done with it.' Harding then turned his attention back to Ethan. 'I need you to make a formal statement. We can do it in the car. It shouldn't take long.'

'Okay, sure,' Ethan handed his bag to Dixel. 'Can you look after this for me?' Normally Dixel would have told him to look after his own stuff, but he looked at her for a split second longer than usual, so she played along.

It took twenty-minutes for officer Harding to be done with him and by then almost everyone had left apart from a couple of officers waiting for forensics to do their sweep. The bittersweetness was everyone had a good time but him. He barely got to put his feet on a board all day.

As he left, he spotted Elliott arguing with his old man. His dad was furious at having his time wasted. Ethan put his hands in his pockets and felt the money he'd taken from Priestley's stash. There was more than enough for himself and Elliott.

'Hey, I've got something for you.'

'Get lost, Wares,' Elliott snapped back.

'I said I'd help you out.' Ethan took out the contents of one pocket. 'The event was more successful than I'd hoped so I want you to have this.'

Surprise slows the mind of people who can't believe their fortunes can turn around so quickly. Ethan felt like an idiot holding out that money until Elliott took it. He was speechless, but his old man spoke for him.

'Well, what do you know? It looks like you've got some friends, after all.'

'It's for your board company. You can buy your stock.'

'Really?' Muscles cramped as thoughts juddered out through his jaw. 'Why?' then 'Thanks. You didn't have to...'

Ethan shrugged.

Elliott took out his phone and called up the

webpage for his board order, then handed all the money to his dad. 'There you go. Five hundred.'

'It's about that,' Ethan confirmed.

'Can you buy it on your bank card?'

His dad took one look at the notes and saw all the day's losses evaporate. He couldn't take his credit card out fast enough and place that board order. They even had it sent to Ethan's flat so Elliott wouldn't have to collect it from his old man's place. He thanked Ethan again, but his old man didn't. He got back in the car and told Elliott to make his own way home, then drove off in the direction of the bookies.

18

LUMP SUM

The following morning Heston and Ethan arranged to meet at Highland Park. It was quiet, just dog walkers and a council truck emptying the bins. Over the last twenty-four hours, Ethan thought of nothing other than the crazy chemist, getting accepted back into his friend circle, his dealings with the EA officers, and the police. It had been a wild few days that he didn't want to repeat. This morning he had another worry: N27. He hadn't provided any footage, which would have earned him a three-strikes disciplinary. Usually, he couldn't care for anything Human Resources did to him, but it all mounted up. The viewings hadn't been high enough and his ratings had slumped. Ricard's Line-life segment had been doing so well that all resources had been directed to his edits. Ethan could only complain so much about the locations and the struggles he'd had, but people were voting with their clicks.

Despite feeling a bit lost, he noticed something else. His *Slings and Arrows* were gone. He'd been thinking clearer, and he couldn't care what N27 did to him anymore. Sure, they'll slap his wrist, but so what?

Across the park, the council truck pulled up alongside a bin and a man in a florescent jacket jumped out and emptied it. Emptying bins wouldn't be too bad a job. The council worker seemed happy enough, probably because no-one bothered him. Driving around all the parks every day was easy work. If N27 prevented him from skating, he'd find a way. Big deal.

When Heston arrived by taxi, Ethan had cheered up a little bit. The autumn breeze had blown the dumb thoughts from between his ears and there was a vague future of something new ahead.

'You look cheerful,' Ethan said. Heston put his crutches on the side of the bench, sat down, and handed over an envelope.

'What's this?'

'No-idea. Open it.'

'I've got a surprise for you.' Ethan pulled out the brick of twenty-pound notes from his bag and set it down on the seat between them.

'Jesus! How much is here?'

'I haven't exactly counted it, but it's everything minus the five-hundred I gave Elliott. It's for you, for the flat, and everything you've done. It should wipe my debt clean.'

'This is police evidence, right?'

Ethan shrugged.

'I mean, they must be looking for it?'

'I don't think they knew how much Priestley had. My guess is it's laundered. Technically free. Invisible. How are they going to trace it?' Ethan said.

'Marked bills or something?' The weight of the brick felt good in Heston's hands.

'I think you've watched too many films.' Ethan sat back and watched the bin man drive across the park and empty another.

'Well, I've got to admit I'm liking this new Ethan.' Heston put the brick back down on the bench. 'It seems like you're acting a bit more responsibly. This is more than enough to cover my medical bills. Between this and the money I've got saved we could use it to get out of here.'

'The Park?'

'No, this town. Haven't you had enough of it?'

'I thought you were buying a house?'

Heston didn't respond. He just raised his eyebrows and shrugged back at his brother. Buying a house was the biggest purchase of someone's life, yet he seemed so nonchalant. Ethan expected him to be a bit happier about it. Maybe a lifetime of bricks and mortar wasn't all it's cracked up to be.

'So, do you know what the latest news is about my job?'

'Your P60 is already in the post'

'P60?'

'Your good-bye letter. If they haven't contacted you yet, they will. And yes, before you ask, the anti-competition clause has been activated.'

'Can I still put edits on YouTube?'

'We'll have to read over your contract, but I wouldn't chance it. There's so much monetisation online, that Legal will be on your back before you know it. Whatever you do, they'll assume there's a personal benefit with a company somewhere down the line and it'll cost you in court to prove there isn't. It'll be easier to just get another job.' Then Heston thought for a moment. 'Actually, don't.' He nodded at the money. 'Take that back. I don't need it.'

'Just accept the damn money,' Ethan said.

As the council truck parked up behind their seats, the worker jumped out to empty their bin. A news report came from the radio. Ethan jumped into the truck and turned it up.

A large, organised crime ring has been discovered south of the city counterfeiting nearly half a million pounds. Police are warning local businesses to check all sums of twenty-pound notes. All banks in the city have been notified. Eight people have been arrested, though much of the money has been collected by the public during the arrest. Police are appealing for people to return any sums they may have received to help with the investigation.

That money-brick instantly became worthless.

19

BURN, BURN

The glowing banknotes crackled and spat in the bin. Heston squinted into the smoke and poked the paper lump with a stick. Even if they had a bucket of water, it was too late to rescue it.

There were no identifiable marks on the letter Ethan held. He ripped it open and tried to read the legalese.

'Anything important?' Heston asked.

'I'm not sure. I think it's from a lawyer.' Ethan scanned over the lines and realised that it was from the office of Dominic Borocca. His secretary had been instructed to fulfil a request from Borocca's first call out of the clinic.

'Let me take a look.'

They exchanged positions: Ethan continued prodding the bin's contents, whilst Heston read, then laughed.

'What does it say?'

It outlined Ethan's contract terms—leaving by his own choice or being sacked would be upheld in UK Courts—however, Borocca's company had discovered the terms would be in breach of his European Rights.

'Under EU Law a company cannot stop you from earning an income from your sole skill, which is skateboarding, because, let's face it, you have no other useful skills.'

'What does that mean?'

Heston read on. 'The European Court of Justice would completely overrule N27s anti-competition clause. The EU has precedents in place to protect all employees from, and I quote, *Denying the ability to earn an income*.' Heston folded up the letter and handed it back to his brother. 'So that's it. You can do whatever you like. They can't stop you.'

'Really?'

'Really.'

'Hell, yes!' Ethan shouted up into the sky. 'I can't believe it. I barely spoke to this guy for like ten drunken minutes. He's just freed me from everything. Now I can do whatever I like?'

'You were drunk?'

'No, he was.' Ethan chucked the stick into the bin and let everything burn. 'Does it say anything about money?'

'You'll get severance pay, back pay, any holiday

pay owed, over time, as well as pension contributions released into a private fund.'

'How much?'

'They'll have to calculate it, but my guess is around twenty-k plus. They're also happy to sue N27 on your behalf—no-win, no-fee—for unfair dismissal, which could bump up the final figure by a lot.'

Ethan jumped around hollering and laughing into the air. When he finally calmed down and took a seat, he still couldn't believe it. He was so thankful for those few minutes off-loading his woes onto Borocca. He wasn't even sure at the time if he was heard. He promised to contact Borocca after a few months to see if he'd dried out and to say thank you.

Heston read over his house agreement.

'So, are you going to sign that then, or what?'

It was clear the estate agent pressure wasn't helping his decision. Something didn't feel right, which Heston couldn't shake. The home would give him the space he wanted away from his brother, but, right now, a contractual noose around his neck felt like the wrong thing. What *he* needed, what they *both* needed was a holiday. He held the contract out over the flames. The corner caught and burnt back on itself into a fragile leaf of blackened ash. Once he couldn't hold it any longer, he released it, and it flipped over rising in the updraft above them. When the ash disappeared behind a tree, Ethan felt both their lives had simplified and his brother wouldn't be returning to work tomorrow.

'You want to go and listen to Dixel's band practice in The Vkng?' Ethan wondered.

'Sure. What sort of music do they play?'

'I don't know, but it's loud and the keyboard player is hot.'

'Is the feeling mutual?'

'I don't think so,' Ethan said.

As they reached the edge of the park, Heston stopped at the gate. He didn't know which direction to head. 'That sofa of yours. How comfortable is it to sleep on?'

'No idea. You want to try it?'

'Yeah. I think I do.'

OTHER TITLES

Read the rest of the Ethan Wares Skateboard series now:

Book 1: The Blocks
Book 2: Abandoned
Book 3: Pool Staker
Book 4: Punch Drunk

AUTHOR'S NOTE

If you liked this story and would be interested in reading more, you can join my mailing list at https://skatefiction.co.uk and become one of my beta readers who get early access to new stories, give feedback, and receive reader copies in advance.

If you loved the book, please leave a positive review wherever you purchased it as this is the main way good books spread and help people discover me.

Thanks - Mark

ABOUT THE AUTHOR

Mark Mapstone is a UK skateboarder, writer, and author of the Ethan Wares Skateboard Series books.

After discovering there were no fiction books written for skateboarders with realistic skateboarding in them, and being qualified with a degree in creative writing from the prestigious Bath Spa University, Mark decided he was perfectly positioned to cater this audience.

In-between road-trips, an infinite Instagram feed of videos to watch, and discovering bruises on himself which he has no-idea how they got there, Mark uses his knowledge of the current skateboarding world to create exciting and authentic stories which every skateboarder goes through daily.

Follow Mark on Instagram: @7plywood.

© 2021 Mark Mapstone

Published by Credible Ink Publishing

Forth edition

No part of this publication may be reproduced, stored or transmitted in any form or by any means, electronic, mechanical, photocopying, recording, scanning, or otherwise without written permission from the publisher. It is illegal to copy this book, post it to a website, or distribute it by any other means without permission. This novel is entirely a work of fiction. The names, characters and incidents portrayed in it are the work of the author's imagination. Any resemblance to actual persons, living or dead, events or localities is entirely coincidental. Mark Mapstone asserts the moral right to be identified as the author of this work.

All rights reserved.

Printed in Great Britain
by Amazon